The End Times

Discovering What the Bible Says

E. MICHAEL RUSTEN

FISHERMAN
BIBLE STUDY SERIES

The End Times

PUBLISHED BY WATERBROOK PRESS
12265 Oracle Boulevard, Suite 200
Colorado Springs, Colorado 80921
A division of Random House, Inc.

All Scripture quotations are taken from the *Holy Bible, New International Version®*. NIV®. Copyright © 1973, 1978, 1984 by International Bible Society. Used by permission of Zondervan Publishing House. All rights reserved.

10 Digit ISBN: 0-87788-234-7
13 Digit ISBN: 978-0-87788-234-3

Printed in the United States of America
2006

10 9 8

Contents

How to Use This Studyguide

Fisherman studyguides are based on the inductive approach to Bible study. Inductive study is discovery study; we discover what the Bible says as we ask questions about its content and search for answers. This is quite different from the process in which a teacher *tells* a group *about* the Bible—what it means and what to do about it. In inductive study, God speaks directly to each of us through his Word.

A group functions best when a leader keeps the discussion on target, but the leader is neither the teacher nor the "answer person." A leader's responsibility is to *ask*—not *tell*. The answers come from the text itself as group members examine, discuss, and think together about the passage.

There are four kinds of questions in each study. The first is an *approach question.* Asked and answered before the Bible passage is read, this question breaks the ice and helps you start thinking about the topic of the Bible study. It begins to reveal where thoughts and feelings need to be transformed by Scripture.

Some of the earlier questions in each study are *observation questions*—who, what, where, when, and how—designed to help you learn some basic facts about the passage of Scripture.

Once you know what the Bible says, you need to ask, *What does it mean?* These *interpretation questions* help you discover the writer's basic message.

Next come *application questions,* which ask, *What does it mean to me?* They challenge you to live out the Scripture's life-transforming message.

Fisherman studyguides provide spaces between questions for jotting down responses as well as any related questions you would like to raise in the group. Each group member should have a copy of the studyguide and may take a turn in leading the group.

A group should use any accurate, modern translation of the Bible such as the *New International Version,* the *New American Standard Bible,* the *New Living Translation,* the *New Revised Standard Version,* the *New Jerusalem Bible,* or the *Good News Bible.* (Other translations or paraphrases of the Bible may be referred to when additional help is needed.) In general, Bible commentaries should not be relied on heavily in a Bible study because they tend to dampen discussion and keep people from thinking for themselves.

Suggestions for Group Leaders

1. Thoroughly read and study the Bible passage before the meeting. Get a firm grasp on its themes and begin applying its teachings for yourself. Pray that the Holy Spirit will "guide you into all truth" (John 16:13) so that your leadership will guide others.

2. If any of the studyguide's questions seem ambiguous or unnatural to you, rephrase them, feeling free to add others that seem necessary to bring out the meaning of a verse.

3. Begin (and end) the study promptly. Start by asking someone to pray that every participant will both understand the passage and be open to its transforming power. Remember, the Holy Spirit is the teacher, not you!

4. Ask for volunteers to read the passages aloud.

5. As you ask the studyguide's questions in sequence, encourage everyone to participate in the discussion. If some are silent, try gently suggesting, "Let's have an answer from someone who hasn't spoken up yet."

6. If a question comes up that you can't answer, don't be afraid to admit that you're baffled. Assign the topic as a research project for someone to report on next week, or say, "I'll do some studying and let you know what I find out."

7. Keep the discussion moving, but be sure it stays focused. Though a certain number of tangents are inevitable, you'll want to quickly bring the discussion back to the topic at hand. Also, learn to pace the discussion so that you finish the lesson in the time allotted.

8. Don't be afraid of silences; some questions take time to answer, and some people need time to gather courage to speak. If silence persists, rephrase your question, but resist the temptation to answer it yourself.

9. If someone comes up with an answer that is clearly illogical or unbiblical, ask for further clarification: "What verse suggests that to you?"

10. Discourage overuse of cross references. Learn all you can from the passage at hand, while selectively incorporating a few important references suggested in the studyguide.

11. Some questions are marked with a ♂. This indicates that further information is available in the Leader's Notes at the back of the guide.

12. For more information on getting a new Bible study group started and keeping it functioning effectively, read *You Can Start a Bible Study Group* by Gladys M. Hunt and *Pilgrims in Progress: Growing Through Groups* by Jim and Carol Plueddemann. (Both books are available from Shaw Books.)

SUGGESTIONS FOR GROUP MEMBERS

1. Learn and apply the following ground rules for effective Bible study. (If new members join the group later, review these guidelines with the whole group.)

2. Remember that your goal is to learn all you can *from the Bible passage being studied.* Let it speak for itself without using Bible commentaries or other Bible passages. There is more than enough in each assigned passage to keep your group productively occupied for one session. Sticking to the passage saves the group from insecurity ("I don't have the right reference books—or the time to read anything else.") and confusion ("Where did *that* come from? I thought we were studying _____.").

3. Avoid the temptation to bring up those fascinating tangents that don't really grow out of the passage you are discussing. If the topic is of common interest, you can bring it up later in informal conversation after the study. Meanwhile, help one another stick to the subject.

4. Encourage one another to participate. People remember best what they discover and verbalize for

themselves. Some people are naturally shy, while others may be afraid of making a mistake. If your discussion is free and friendly and you show real interest in what other group members think and feel, the quieter ones will be more likely to speak up. Remember, the more people involved in a discussion, the richer it will be.

5. Guard yourself from answering too many questions or talking too much. Give others a chance to share their ideas. If you are one who participates easily, discipline yourself by counting to ten before you open your mouth.

6. Make personal, honest applications and commit yourself to letting God's Word change you.

Introduction

Why study the end times? Christians give diverse answers to this question. For some people, to study the end times is to investigate the background of daily news headlines as possible fulfillments of biblical prophecy. Others feel that if theologians can't agree about what is going to happen in connection with the second coming of Christ, there is no point in trying to figure things out for themselves. No matter where you are on this spectrum of interest, the fact is that God has revealed, in part, the future to us. We are therefore to endeavor to understand it as we do the rest of his revelation in Scripture.

Both the Old and New Testaments contain prophecies of the end of the age. The Old Testament prophets often prophesied about the distant future. Many of their prophecies were fulfilled at Christ's first coming, while the fulfillment of others awaits the end of the age. In the New Testament, Jesus himself gave an extended overview of the events leading up to his second coming in what is known as the Olivet Discourse (Mark 13:5-37; Luke 21:8-36), with Matthew devoting two full chapters to his account (Matthew 24–25). Many Christians understand the last book of the Bible, the book of Revelation, to be devoted almost entirely to an account of the end times.

What we can conclude is that God, as the author of both the Bible and history, has chosen to reveal to us in outline his plan for history—the future as well as the past. God considered it important for his people to realize that he is the victor in the conflict of the ages and that he will surely accomplish all his purposes.

What complicates our study of the end times is that much of it is described in a symbolic style of writing called *apocalyptic*. Whereas this type of literature was familiar to many of the original readers of the Old and New Testaments, it sounds very strange to our modern ears. Much of the books of Ezekiel, Daniel, Joel, and Zechariah were written in apocalyptic form, as was the book of Revelation. In addition, during the period between the Testaments, a number of Jewish apocalyptic books were written describing the coming of the kingdom of God. For us to make sense of the language of prophecy, we need to keep several principles in mind as we study these passages.

First of all, God's purpose in the Scriptures is to reveal truth to us, not to confuse us. Therefore, we need to concentrate on the truths that we do understand and not become frustrated by the details that are still confusing to us.

A second basic principle involves how symbols are to be interpreted. We can interpret a symbol literally by determining what it symbolizes. The meanings of most of the symbols of the Bible are either explained somewhere in Scripture or have cultural explanations. So it is up to us to find the other usages of a symbol in the Bible to determine what is being symbolized. To ascertain whether a symbol has a historical or cultural background, you may want to have a Bible dictionary or Bible commentary handy as you do this study. I've also provided some background information in the Leader's Notes for your reference.

A third principle for interpreting Bible prophecies is to compare Scripture with Scripture. The Bible is the best interpreter of itself. We should look up cross references and study as many passages as we can that discuss the subject we are investigating.

The fourth and probably the most crucial principle for studying the end times is that we need to understand God's purpose in revealing these truths to us. God did not reveal the future to us to tickle our intellects or to satisfy our curiosity. There will not be a reward in heaven for the person who has the best end-times chart. God has shown us how he will conclude history *in order to change our lives.* At the beginning of the book of Revelation, John wrote, "Blessed is the one who reads the words of this prophecy, and blessed are those who hear it and take to heart what is written in it" (1:3). God has revealed the future so that we will "take it to heart" and give him our total allegiance.

Finally, we must prayerfully study the end-times references in Scripture, asking the Holy Spirit to be our teacher and lead us into all truth.

An Overview
of the End Times

MATTHEW 24:1-31

Human beings seem to have an insatiable interest in knowing things ahead of time. From weather and traffic-flow reports to psychic hotlines, we all want to know the future. Christians have questions too: Are we living in the last days? Could Christ come today? Is a particular headline a sign of the times? But rather than checking a horoscope, we can go to the Bible. Matthew, Mark, and Luke give us an overview of the end times along with a discussion of the events leading up to Christ's second coming. In this first study, we'll look at Matthew's account.

Bible-believing Christians do not all agree on the details of the end times. Therefore, if you are doing this study in a group, you may find differences of interpretation among group members. What is important is that you try to let the text speak for itself and at the same time be accepting of the opinions of others. Our goal is the same: to gain a deeper understanding of Scripture and to let its truths change our lives.

1. What are one or two main questions you hope to answer for yourself in this study on the end times?

READ MATTHEW 24:1-14.

🖋 2. What prompted the disciples' questions? What did they specifically want to know?

3. What events did Jesus say will characterize the period described in verses 4-8?

What descriptive phrase did Jesus use? What does it convey (verse 8)?

4. Why will Christians be persecuted during these times (verses 9-14)?

Do you think Christians should prepare for persecution and possible martyrdom? If so, how?

5. What can we do to stand firm and make sure we are not among those who will "turn away from the faith" (verse 10)?

6. According to verse 14, what is the relationship, if any, between foreign missions and the second coming of Christ?

READ MATTHEW 24:15-25.

7. In verse 15 the expression "the abomination that causes desolation" probably refers to a desecration of a temple, "the holy place." What do you gather from this passage about the meaning and import of this event?

8. What do you think it will be like to be a believer living in the time of unequaled great distress (verses 21-24)?

9. Why do you think Jesus told us these things "ahead of time"?

READ MATTHEW 24:26-31.

10. What did Jesus say will distinguish his coming from the coming of false Christs (verses 23-31)?

11. Describe what Jesus's second coming will look like (verses 30-31). What does this picture tell us about who Jesus is?

12. What is your reaction to these signs of the end of the age? What specific applications do you think God wants you to make to your life based on this study?

Passages for further study: Daniel 2:31-45; 7:1-27; 9:24-27; Mark 13:1-27; Luke 21:5-28; Revelation 6:1–7:17.

When Will Christ Return?

Matthew 24:32–25:13

Jesus's disciples captured the curiosity of us all when they inquired, "Lord, what will be the sign of your coming and of the end of the age?" In other words, "Just lay it out for us in black and white, please." Fortunately, Jesus answered their question, and he did so in two ways. First, he summarized the events of the end times that we studied in the last lesson. Fairly black-and-white. Then he told some stories—parables—that shed more light and color on the question of when he would return.

1. Do you expect to live to see the second coming of the Lord Jesus Christ? Why or why not?

READ MATTHEW 24:32-41.

🖊 2.   To what do the phrases "all these things" and "it is
        near" refer (verse 33)? How do you know?

   3.   According to verses 32 and 33, will believers living
        in the end times be able to know when to expect the
        Second Coming? Why or why not?

   4.   What do you think "this generation" refers to: Jesus's
        own generation or the generation that will "see all
        these things" (verses 33-34)? Explain.

        What assurance does Jesus provide us in the midst
        of uncertain times?

🖊 5.   How can we reconcile the seemingly contradictory
        ideas in verses 33 and 36?

6. According to verses 37-41, what will life be like for unbelievers in the days leading up to the Second Coming?

↗ 7. What is being referred to by the phrase "one will be taken" (verses 40-41)?

READ MATTHEW 24:42-51.

8. What point did Jesus reiterate throughout these parables? Why do you think this is so important?

9. What did the faithful servant and the wicked servant have in common? How were they different?

READ MATTHEW 25:1-13.

⚡ 10. What is the main lesson of the parable of the ten virgins?

11. What does it mean to you to "keep watch" and be ready for the coming of Christ?

12. What can you do during the next week to apply the lessons of these parables to your life?

Passages for further study: Mark 13:28-37; Luke 21:28-36; Acts 1:7; Revelation 2:1–3:22.

The Antichrist and the Great Tribulation

MATTHEW 24:4-29; SELECTIONS FROM
REVELATION 13–17; DANIEL 7:1-7

From fake money to false advertising, the danger of counterfeits is everywhere. It looks real, it feels real, it sounds legitimate. But in the end, counterfeits have no substance. The Bible speaks of the fact that a counterfeit Christ—the Antichrist—is coming. He will be the ultimate con artist who will oppose Christ and his kingdom. In addition, there will be a "great tribulation," an expression used in some Bible translations for the time of great distress and persecution referred to in Matthew 24:21 and Revelation 7:14.

The passages we look at today are difficult ones and not easy to understand. The important thing is to get the big picture and be assured once again of God's hand in history.

1. Have you ever experienced persecution as a Christian? If so, what lesson(s) did you learn from that experience?

Read Matthew 24:4-29.

2. What do you learn about the false Christs in verses 4-5 and 23-26?

3. From the context in this passage, do you think the "great distress" or "great tribulation" refers to a time in the future or to the present church age in which we live? Give reasons for your answer.

Read Revelation 13:1-2 and Daniel 7:1-7.

4. Who is the Dragon referred to in Revelation 13:1-2 (review Revelation 12:9)?

5. Note the images of the beasts in these two passages. In what ways are they similar? (Compare Revelation 13:1 with Daniel 7:7, and Revelation 13:2 with Daniel 7:4-6.)

What can we learn from these similarities about the identity of the Beast?

READ REVELATION 13:3-10 AND 17:9-11.

6. Without trying to understand all the details, in general what does 17:9-11 say the heads represent? (This passage gives an interpretation of the seven heads of the Beast referred to in Revelation 13:1-3 and 17:3. See leader's note for more information.)

7. Summarize the role of the Beast (13:3-10). What is the secret to his success? How long will his success last?

READ REVELATION 13:11-18 AND 14:9-12.

8. The second beast of 13:11-18 is later called "the false prophet" in Revelation 19:20. Why might he be given this designation?

Describe the activities of the false prophet.

9. What will be the source of the miraculous power of the false prophet?

    How might these verses affect how we regard miraculous events today?

10. What is the penalty for those who refuse to worship the Antichrist (13:15)? How do you feel about the possibility that you might someday be martyred for your faith in Christ?

11. Why do you think there are such strong warnings in 14:9-10 against worshiping the Beast or receiving his mark?

THE ANTICHRIST AND THE GREAT TRIBULATION

12. Revelation 13 describes a trinity of evil: the Dragon (Satan), the first beast (the Antichrist), and second beast (the false prophet). In what sense is this trinity a counterfeit of the divine Trinity? List as many similarities as you can between the roles of the persons of the trinity of evil and the roles of the Father, Son, and Holy Spirit.

13. Since no one knows which generation will experience the events of Revelation 13, what can we do to prepare ourselves in case we are that generation?

Passages for further study: Daniel 7:8-25; Matthew 24:15-28; Mark 13:14-23; 2 Thessalonians 2:1-12.

The Second Coming of Christ

JOHN 14:1-6; ACTS 1:1-11; 1 THESSALONIANS 3:13; 4:13-18

The second coming of the Lord Jesus Christ will be the most glorious event of human history. Christians in every age have looked forward to that time when Christ will return on the clouds of heaven. Though Christians hold different opinions on the timing of Christ's return, we have the assurance that he will indeed come. It is our ultimate hope. Billy Graham has observed, "Our world is filled with fear, hate, lust, greed, war, and utter despair. Surely the second coming of Jesus Christ is the only hope of replacing these features with trust, love, universal peace, and prosperity. For it the world wittingly or inadvertently waits."

✎ 1. How and where did you come to your present understanding of what occurs at the second coming of Christ?

READ JOHN 14:1-6.

✎ 2. Where did Jesus say the believer will be taken (verses 2-3)? What can we learn from Jesus's use of the expression "my Father's house"?

3. When Jesus said, "I will come back and take you to be with me," do you think he was referring to the believer's death, to his second coming, or to both? Explain.

4. Compare verses 4 and 6. What did Jesus mean when he said, "the way to the place where I am going"? How is Jesus "the way"?

READ ACTS 1:1-11.

5. List as many similarities as you can between the ascension of Jesus and his second coming.

READ 1 THESSALONIANS 3:13 AND 4:13-18.

6. What further light does 3:13 shed on the second coming of Christ?

✍ 7. What practical concern of the Thessalonian Christians was Paul addressing in 4:13-14?

What is most encouraging to you in this passage?

8. In what ways do we as Christians view death differently from unbelievers?

🖋 9. What does 4:14-17 tell us about the order of events at Christ's return?

10. In study 1 we examined Jesus's account of his return. Compare Matthew 24:30-31 and 1 Thessalonians 4:16-17. Are these passages describing the same event or different events? Explain your answer.

11. Why do you think both 4:17 and John 14:3 emphasize our being "with" the Lord?

12. In what ways does knowing that Jesus is coming
     back affect your life today?

Pray for one another to be strong, blameless, and holy as you
joyfully anticipate Christ's return.

Passages for further study: Mark 13:24-27; Luke 21:25-27; Revelation 1:7; 14:14-16; 19:11-16.

The Resurrection of the Dead

1 CORINTHIANS 15:1-58

In our culture, Easter has come to be associated with spring and bunnies and colored eggs, not the truth of the resurrection of Jesus. But the resurrection of the dead is a profound truth revealed in the Bible from the earliest times. Job stated, "I know that my Redeemer lives, and that in the end he will stand upon the earth. And after my skin has been destroyed, yet in my flesh I will see God" (Job 19:25-26).

In the New Testament, the preaching of the apostles centered on the resurrection of Jesus. This was the theme of Peter's sermon on the Day of Pentecost. The preaching and teaching of the Resurrection distinguished the early Christians from other religions that had only tales of mythological resurrections. In stark contrast, the apostles preached a Christ whose death and resurrection they had personally witnessed. Not only did Jesus rise from the dead, but he taught that both believers and unbelievers would also experience resurrection.

1. What is your favorite Easter memory? Does Jesus's resurrection have a part in this memory? Explain.

READ 1 CORINTHIANS 15:1-11.

2. According to Paul, what constitutes the gospel?

3. Why do you think Paul mentioned the more than five hundred people to whom Jesus appeared?

   How does this influence your understanding of the reality of Jesus's resurrection?

READ 1 CORINTHIANS 15:12-34.

4. What heresy was Paul addressing in these verses?

   What was Paul's attitude toward those who held this heresy?

✐ 5. In what ways is the Resurrection crucial to the Christian faith?

✐ 6. At what times in history will there be a resurrection (verses 20-24)?

What further light does Revelation 20:4-5 shed on this question?

7. What do we learn in verses 24-28 about how God will end human history?

READ 1 CORINTHIANS 15:35-49.

8. From this passage, how would you answer in your own words the questions Paul raised in verse 35?

9. List as many contrasts as you can between Adam and Christ (verses 21-22,45-49). What is the significance of these contrasts?

READ 1 CORINTHIANS 15:50-58.

10. Do you think verses 51 and 52 are referring to the same event that is described in 1 Thessalonians 4:13-17? in Matthew 24:30-31? Why or why not?

11. How does God achieve his ultimate purposes of reestablishing his kingdom and subduing his enemies (verses 22-28,50-58)?

12. What does Christ's resurrection mean to you personally? What does the resurrection of the dead mean to you?

Passages for further study: Matthew 28:1-15; Mark 16:1-8; Luke 24:1-49; John 20:1-29; 1 Thessalonians 4:13-18; Revelation 20:4-6.

God's Plan for Israel

ROMANS 11:1-36

Almost daily the nation of Israel is in the news. There is no other small nation in the world that continually attracts as much international attention as does Israel. Christians are in basic agreement about the nation of Israel in Old Testament history. God called Abraham from Ur of the Chaldeans to the land of Canaan, which God promised to Abraham's descendants. Abraham's grandson was Jacob, whose name was changed to Israel. The twelve tribes of Israel are the descendants of Jacob's twelve sons. Then, at Mount Sinai, God made the twelve tribes into "a kingdom of priests and a holy nation" (Exodus 19:6).

The manner in which the Old Testament prophecies regarding Israel will be fulfilled is what Christians disagree about. Are these prophecies to be fulfilled in the nation of Israel or are they presently being fulfilled by the church? We cannot cover this topic completely, but let's begin by examining Romans 11, a key chapter on this subject.

1. Why do you think the nation of Israel attracts so much attention today?

READ ROMANS 11:1-24.

2. In Romans 10 Paul discussed how the Israelites had hardened their hearts to the gospel. Yet what proof did Paul offer to support his claim that God has not rejected his people (verses 1-5)?

3. Note how Paul identified God's people in verse 5. What does this description reveal about God (verses 4-6)?

4. Who do the branches that have been broken off represent (verses 17-20)? Why were they were broken off?

5. What does the wild olive shoot represent (verse 17)? What does the cultivated olive tree represent (verse 24)? How did you reach your conclusions?

6. What do verses 23 and 24 tell us regarding a future for Israel?

READ ROMANS 11:25-32.

✐ 7. Paul reached the climax of his teaching regarding Israel in these verses. Summarize what he was saying.

✐ 8. How does Paul's use of the Old Testament support the point he was making (verses 26-27)?

✐ 9. Read Zechariah 12:10 and Revelation 1:7. On whom is the Spirit poured out in Zechariah 12:10? What happens when the Spirit is poured out?

✐ 10. What is the significance of the fact that Revelation 1:7 quotes Zechariah 12:10? Are there any parallels here to Romans 11:26-27?

11. What place, if any, do you believe that Jews and the State of Israel have in God's plan for the future? What are the main reasons for your conclusion?

READ ROMANS 11:33-36.

12. What was Paul's reaction to the truths he had just discussed in these verses? What did he conclude?

Close your time together in prayer and praise, using the doxology in Romans as a starting point.

Passages for further study: Genesis 17:1-13; Jeremiah 31:31-40; Ezekiel 20:1-44; 37:1-28; Luke 1:30-33; Revelation 7:1-8.

The Day of the Lord and the Wrath of God

1 THESSALONIANS 5:1-11; 2 THESSALONIANS 2:1-4;
JOEL 2:31-32; REVELATION 15:1–16:11

G od says of his enemies, "It is mine to avenge;…their day of disaster is near and their doom rushes upon them" (Deuteronomy 32:35). People around us may seem to not experience the consequences of their behavior, but there is coming a day when they will reap what they have sown. The expression "Day of the Lord" is frequently used throughout the Bible to describe a time when God visits his wrath and vengeance on those who have opposed him and broken his covenant. God's wrath is sobering, but we can be assured that his judgment is also righteous and just.

The Old Testament records days of the Lord against the nations of Babylon, Edom, Egypt, Moab, and many others. God will also have a day against Israel. All of these days of the Lord point forward to the final day of wrath. In this culminating Day of the Lord, "everyone who calls on the name of the Lord will be saved," whereas God will pour out judgment upon his enemies.

1. As you understand it, how can a loving God exhibit wrath?

READ 1 THESSALONIANS 5:1-11.

2. Identify as many details of the Day of the Lord as you can from Paul's description in this passage.

3. Does this passage teach that the Day of the Lord begins with the return of Christ that is mentioned in 1 Thessalonians 4:16-17? Explain your answer.

4. Who will be surprised by the coming of the Day of the Lord? How do you know?

Who will experience the destruction and wrath of God? How do you know?

READ 2 THESSALONIANS 2:1-4.

5. According to this passage, what two events will take place before the coming of the Day of the Lord?

6. What are the implications of this for determining an exact date for the Day of the Lord?

READ JOEL 2:31-32.

7. According to this passage, what will immediately precede the Day of the Lord?

8. To what deliverance might verse 32 be referring? Why do you think so?

READ REVELATION 15:1–16:11.

9. Just prior to the time when God pours out his wrath upon the earth, where are "those who had been victorious over the beast," and what are they doing (15:1-4)?

10. Summarize in your own words the descriptions of the wrath of God in the first five bowls (16:1-11).

   How will unbelieving humanity react to the wrath of God? What does this tell us about the depravity of humankind?

11. Reread question 1. How do 15:3-4 and 16:5-7 answer this question?

   What does this teach you about who God is and his part in history?

12. What lessons can we as believers learn from what the Bible teaches about the Day of the Lord and the wrath of God?

Passages for further study: Isaiah 2:6-22; Malachi 4:1-6; Romans 2:1-11; 2 Peter 3:8-13; Revelation 8:12–9:21; 14:17-20.

The Battle
of Armageddon

JOEL 3:1-21; REVELATION 16:12-16; 19:7-21

A rmageddon is coming soon!" This has been the message of a steady stream of Christian books and articles for decades. The Battle of Armageddon is a subject that intrigues Christians and non-Christians alike. Both world wars have been identified as leading to Armageddon. The rise of communist Russia was understood to be a precursor to this final battle. The formation of the State of Israel in 1948 caused some to predict that within a generation Christ would return for the Battle of Armageddon.

In the midst of all this speculation, what does the Bible actually say about Armageddon? When this battle will occur and what will happen there are the subjects of this study.

1. What is your emotional reaction when you hear the Battle of Armageddon being discussed? Why?

READ JOEL 3:1-21.

  2.   What will be some of the results of this final battle between God and the nations?

  3.   According to this passage, what different roles will God play in this confrontation with the nations?

  4.   What other insights into this battle does this passage provide?

READ REVELATION 16:12-16.

  5.   What is the relationship between this passage and verses 1-11, which we looked at in study 7?

What does this tell us about the timing of the Battle of Armageddon in comparison with other end-times events?

⟋ 6. Try to imagine this ominous scene. What do you see and feel? Identify as many details as you can regarding the Battle of Armageddon.

READ REVELATION 19:7-21.

7. Who is the rider on the white horse?

What does this vision reveal about the second coming of Christ?

8. What do you observe here about the chronological relationship between the second coming of Christ, the wrath of God, and the Battle of Armageddon?

✍ 9. Note the two suppers that are mentioned in verses 7-9 and 17. What do you learn by comparing these two suppers?

10. What might be some of God's purposes for revealing to us the facts about the Battle of Armageddon?

11. How does knowing God's ending to the story affect your life right now?

Passages for further study: Isaiah 34:1-15; Jeremiah 25:30-33; Zechariah 12:1–14:21; Revelation 9:12-20; 17:8-14.

The Judgment Seat of Christ

2 CORINTHIANS 5:1-10; 1 CORINTHIANS 3:6-15;
REVELATION 11:15-18

Popular theology tells us that at the Final Judgment, God will add up all our good works and all of our sins. If we have more good works than sins, we will go to heaven; but if our sins outweigh our good works, we will go to hell. This is correct in one sense: We will all be judged according to our deeds. Yet the Christian's hope is secure. Our sins have been forgiven through Christ's death on the cross, and God says that he will remember them no more.

In his book *Wishful Thinking*, Frederick Buechner observes, "God will ring down the final curtain on history, and there will come a Day on which all our days…and all our judgments upon each other will themselves be judged. The judge will be Christ. In other words, the one who judges us most finally will be the one who loves us most fully."

1. What images come to your mind when you think of standing before the judgment seat of Christ?

READ 2 CORINTHIANS 5:1-10.

2. What is the believer's ultimate hope and confidence?

How do we know this for sure (verses 5-6)?

3. What will happen at the judgment seat of Christ (verse 10)?

In what way did this affect Paul's perspective on life?

4. Does the "we" in verse 10 refer to believers, unbelievers, or both? Why do you think so?

Read 1 Corinthians 3:6-15.

5. What do you think it means to build on the foundation of Jesus Christ (verses 10-11)?

6. Paul listed several possible "building materials" for our lives. What might they represent (verse 12)?

How would each respond to the test of fire?

7. Is anyone pictured as losing his or her salvation in this passage? What are the reasons for your answer?

READ REVELATION 11:15-18.

8. In this scene, what things do the loud voices and elders affirm?

9. When will God's people receive their rewards?

10. What attributes of God are revealed in this scene?

11. How does knowing that you will one day stand before the judgment seat of Christ affect your life here and now?

Passages for further study: Matthew 25:14-46; Luke 19:11-27; 1 Corinthians 9:24-27; 2 Timothy 4:8; Revelation 22:12.

The Millennium

REVELATION 20:1-10

W ill there be a Millennium—a thousand-year reign of Christ over the earth? This is an issue on which Bible-believing Christians differ. There are three basic views regarding the Millennium. The first is called premillennialism, meaning that Christ will return before ("pre") the Millennium. A second view is called postmillennialism, in which Christ returns following ("post") the Millennium. The third viewpoint among Christian interpreters is called amillennialism, which believes that there will be no ("a") Millennium.

Though we can only look briefly at this topic, study with open and prayerful hearts. You may want to determine which of the above views you feel is most in keeping with the teaching of Scripture. No matter which view you take, we can all rejoice in the fact that Christ will surely establish his kingdom!

1. What is the relevance of studying whether or not there will be a Millennium? What difference does it make?

READ REVELATION 20:1-3.

2. Who are the main characters in this scene?

Note the action verbs. What does this tell you about who is in control?

3. Are the events of verses 1-3 related chronologically to the prior passage in 19:11-21? Why or why not?

4. Where and when is Satan bound? Do you think this is happening in the present or is it a future event? Give reasons for your answer.

What would be the practical differences between a world where Satan was bound and a world where Satan was not bound?

5. What do we know about those who were seated on the thrones?

6. What do you think reigning with Christ will entail?

⚡ 7. To what does the "first resurrection" refer (verses 5-6)? Explain your answer.

8. Whom do you think are "the rest of the dead" (verse 5)?

9. Why would God release Satan from his prison?

10. What differences and similarities do you find between this battle and the Battle of Armageddon (19:11-21)? Are they the same battle?

What are the results of this battle?

11. What is your overall impression of the Millennium now?

12. After studying this passage, do you feel that premillennialism, postmillennialism, or amillennialism best explains these verses? Why? (You may want to refer to the summary chart in appendix A.)

Passages for further study: Isaiah 11:1–12:6; Jeremiah 23:3-8; Ezekiel 36:24–37:28; Luke 22:14-30; 1 Corinthians 15:22-28; Revelation 11:15-19.

The Final Judgment

REVELATION 19:1-4; 20:11-15

T he Last Judgment is sometimes referred to as the "great white throne judgment," based on the apostle John's description of his vision in Revelation 20:11. Though most people are adept at ignoring the inevitability of death, all will one day stand before God in judgment. For believers, this will be the most sobering moment of their existence; for unbelievers, it will be the most terrifying. This study will help us come to an understanding of the awesome Final Judgment, with God in his role as righteous judge.

1. What feelings do you experience when a non-Christian friend dies? Why?

READ REVELATION 19:1-4 AND 20:11.

2. Who is the one sitting on the throne? What kind of
    judge is he?

3. According to a related passage, 2 Peter 3:7-13, how
    will the earth and sky flee from God's presence?
    What might that look like?

READ REVELATION 20:12-15.

4. Are the dead described in verses 12 and 13 believers,
    unbelievers, or both? What are the reasons for your
    answer?

    What more do you learn by comparing the passage
    with Revelation 20:5-6?

⚘ 5. The ancient practice of record keeping is analogous to the books of heaven. What is the basis of the judgment of the Great White Throne?

Why do you think judgment is according to *works?*

⚘ 6. What is the significance of the statement "the sea gave up the dead that were in it, and death and Hades gave up the dead that were in them" (verse 13)?

⚘ 7. Who or what will be thrown into the lake of fire?

Why do you suppose the lake of fire is called "the second death"? (Compare also Revelation 20:6.)

8. Are you afraid of death? Why or why not?

9. What do these verses teach us about hell?

10. As you understand it, when will this Final Judgment take place?

11. What truths have particularly struck you from this passage on the Final Judgment? What action does this lead to in your life?

Passages for further study: Genesis 2:17; Matthew 13:24-30,36-43; John 5:21-30; Hebrews 9:27; 10:26-31.

The New Heaven and the New Earth

REVELATION 21:1–22:9

The Bible begins and ends with the theme of God's creation. "In the beginning God created the heavens and the earth," we read in Genesis 1:1. Then in the book of Revelation, John declares, "I saw a new heaven and a new earth, for the first heaven and the first earth had passed away" (21:1). God promises he will make everything new.

In this final study we will look at the goal of history: the new heaven and the new earth, where God will dwell forever with his people. These chapters contain some of the most beautiful and encouraging words in all of Scripture. And the good news is that all those who have put their trust in Jesus will experience the new heaven and the new earth for all eternity.

1. When you think of spending eternity with God, what do you imagine it will be like? What do you think you will spend your time doing?

READ REVELATION 21:1-8.

 2. Search the passage for the following facts and give the reasoning behind your answers.

When will God create the new heaven and the new earth?

Where is the New Jerusalem now, and who lives there?

How is the Holy City described?

Who will inherit all this?

3. List as many blessings of the New Jerusalem as you can from verses 1-7.

Which of these promises is most meaningful to you right now? Why?

Read Revelation 21:9-21.

4. What is written on the gates and foundations of the city (verses 12-14)? Why is that significant?

5. What are the dimensions of the New Jerusalem? What overall impression do you get of the city from these verses?

Read Revelation 21:22–22:5.

6. How does the description here of the New Jerusalem compare with that of the Garden of Eden in Genesis 2–3?

What is the significance of these comparisons for understanding God's ultimate purposes from Creation to the end of history?

7. Who will live in the city, and what will they be doing (21:24-22:5)?

What does verse 27 tell us that will help us understand more about "the kings of the earth [who] will bring their splendor into it"?

8. List the metaphors and poetic images used for description here. How do these pictures affect your view of what eternity will be like in God's presence?

9. Where will believers spend eternity? Explain your answer.

Read Revelation 22:6-9.

10. The angel declared that these words are true and trustworthy. How did John respond to what God revealed about the end times?

11. What is your response to this study of the end times? (What have you learned? How has your view of God changed? How do you want to live in light of these truths?)

12. If you wish, make your own chart of the order of events of the end times as you understand them (see appendix A).

Passages for further study: Isaiah 24:1–25:12; 65:17-25; 66:22-24; Daniel 7:26-27; Hebrews 12:22-24; 2 Peter 3:3-13.

Leader's Notes

STUDY 1: AN OVERVIEW OF THE END TIMES

Question 2. Jesus's prophecy in Matthew 24:2 of the destruction of the temple was fulfilled in AD 70, when the Roman armies captured Jerusalem, destroyed the temple, and took the surviving Jews captive.

The disciples asked not only about when the end times would come but also about when the temple would be destroyed. Some Bible students believe that Luke 21:5-36 answers the disciples' question as it pertains to the coming destruction of the temple, while the Matthew 24 and Mark 13 passages are referring primarily to Christ's second coming and the end of the age. Jesus could answer both questions simultaneously since the events of AD 70 parallel the events of the end of the age. Does that perspective make sense to you?

Question 7. The expression "abomination that causes desolation" is found in Daniel 9:27; 11:31; and 12:11. Daniel 9:27 states that one "will put an end to sacrifice and offering. And on a wing of the temple he will set up an abomination that causes desolation." Some Bible scholars understand this to be a reference to the Antichrist's desecrating a Jewish temple three and one-half years before the second coming of Christ. Other interpreters believe that this refers to the destruction of the temple in Jerusalem by Titus and his Roman armies in AD 70.

Almost all Bible scholars agree that Daniel 11:31 is a prophecy of the Syrian emperor Antiochus IV Epiphanes who, in 168 BC, "erected a desolating sacrilege upon the altar of burnt offering and offered sacrifices upon the altar which was upon the altar of burnt offering" (1 Maccabees 1:54,59; First Maccabees is a Jewish historical book included in the Apocrypha).

The precise interpretation of Daniel 12:11 has puzzled most Bible students.

Question 10. In the Old Testament, the darkening of the sun and the moon is the precursor of the Day of the Lord (see Isaiah 13:9-10; Joel 2:31-32; 3:14-17). A "day of the Lord" is a time when God pours out his wrath and judgments on those who have broken his covenant (Zephaniah 1:14-15). We will study this in more depth in study 7.

STUDY 2: WHEN WILL CHRIST RETURN?

Question 2. The Greek words for "it is near" in Matthew 24:33 can be translated either "it is near" or "he is near." Which translation makes the best sense to you in light of the context?

Question 5. For clarification, it may help to ask, Is Matthew 24:36 referring to the fact that no one can date the Second Coming from a long-term perspective, or that no one actually living in the end times will have any idea when Christ may return, or both?

Question 7. In Matthew 24:39, "the flood came and took them all away," the verb *took away* is from the Greek word *airo,* meaning "take away or remove." In other words, the flood "removed" them all. In Matthew 24:40-41, "one will be taken and the other left," the word translated *taken* is a different verb, *paralambanō,* which means to "take to oneself." In other words, one will be "taken to someone" (Arndt and Gingrich, *A Greek Lexicon of the New Testament and Other Early Christian Literature,* 2nd ed., Chicago: University of Chicago Press, 1979, pp. 24, 619).

Question 10. The Greek word *hupantēsis,* translated "meet" in Matthew 25:1,6 is used in only two other verses in the New Testament: 1 Thessalonians 4:17 and Acts 28:15.

STUDY 3: THE ANTICHRIST AND THE GREAT TRIBULATION

Question 2. The Antichrist is coming, but he will be preceded by many antichrists (1 John 2:18). The Greek preposition *anti* contains both the ideas of opposition ("against") and substitution ("instead of"). Both of these concepts apply to the New Testament Antichrist or Beast.

For an excellent discussion of the meaning of *Antichrist,* see David A. Hubbard's article "Antichrist" in *Bakers Dictionary of Theology* (Grand Rapids: Baker, 1960, pp. 46-48).

Question 3. This period of persecution and suffering is understood by some to refer to the future rule of the Antichrist, while others see the Great Tribulation to be a reference to the time from AD 70 to the present.

Question 4. An important key to interpreting the apocalyptic language of the book of Revelation in general is found in the book's very first verse. Revelation 1:1 states, "The revelation of Jesus Christ, which God gave him to show his servants what must soon take place. He made it known by sending his angel to his servant John." The Greek word *sēmainō*, "made known," literally means "to signify" or "to show by means of symbols." In other words, in the last book of the Bible, Jesus Christ is giving us his revelation, and he will show us his revelation by means of symbols. The way to interpret a symbol literally is to determine what it symbolizes.

Question 5. Daniel 7 is a parallel prophecy to Daniel 2. Both chapters are prophecies of four successive kingdoms or empires that will dominate the earth from Daniel's time until the coming of the kingdom of God (7:17-18). Most Bible scholars understand that the first beast (7:4) represents the Babylonian Empire (626–539 BC); the second beast (7:5), the Medo-Persian Empire (539–330 BC); the third beast (7:6), the Greek Empire (330–63 BC); and the fourth beast (7:7), the Roman Empire (63 BC–AD 476).

Question 6. Many interpreters understand the term *beast* used in Revelation 13:1-2 as an allusion to the "beasts" of Daniel 7. But many believe that, beginning in Revelation 13:3, the "beast" refers to the other head "of the beast [which] seemed to have had a fatal wound, but the fatal wound had been healed" (Revelation 13:3). Many scholars identify this beast of 13:3-10 as the Antichrist. Do these interpretations make sense to you? Why or why not?

Question 7. A three-and-one-half-year period is also mentioned in Revelation 11:2-3 and 12:6. The expression "time, times and half a time" used in Daniel 7:25 and quoted in Revelation 12:14 means literally three and one-half times. In Daniel 7:25

"times" has a dual ending in Aramaic, indicating two times. So the expression "time, times and half a time" means 1 time + 2 times + $\frac{1}{2}$ a time (or, again, a total of $3\frac{1}{2}$ times). In Revelation 12:14, this phrase is parallel to "1,260 days" (12:6) or three and one-half years.

Question 11. In the ancient world, religious tattoos on the hand or forehead were common, indicating one's allegiance to a particular god.

Since the Greeks did not have written numbers as we do, they assigned numerical values to each letter of their alphabet. As a result, people would know the numerical value of their names. For example, on a wall of Pompeii was found written, "I love her whose number is 545." Therefore, many Bible scholars believe that the numerical value of the Antichrist's name will be 666, while others understand 666 to be a demonic parody of the perfect number 777. By contrast, Revelation 14:1 and 22:4 indicate that after Jesus's second coming, the redeemed will have God's name on their foreheads.

For a further discussion of the mark of the Beast, see N. J. Opperwald, "Mark," in *The International Standard Bible Encyclopedia,* rev. ed., (Grand Rapids: Eerdmans, 1986, 3:248) and George R. Beasley-Murray, "Revelation," in the *New Bible Commentary, 21st Century Edition* (Downers Grove, IL: InterVarsity, 1994, p. 1443).

STUDY 4: THE SECOND COMING OF CHRIST

Question 1. Since you may find differences of opinion on the subject of the Second Coming within your study group, you may want to remind your group of the Bible's principles of what to do when Christians disagree on issues not crucial to the Christian faith. In Romans 14 Paul devoted a whole chapter to this question. His principles included:

1. Accept one another (verse 1).
2. Don't judge your brother (verses 3-11).
3. Be fully convinced in your own mind (verse 5).

Question 2. In a Jewish wedding ceremony, the groom, accompanied by relatives and friends, came out to meet the bride and escort her back to his house or to his father's house, where elaborate preparations had been made for the wedding feast. What a wonderful picture of heaven!

Question 7. The Scriptures frequently use *sleep* as an expression for death (see Job 14:10-12; John 11:11-14; 1 Corinthians 15:18). However, this figure of speech alludes to the *body* as sleeping after death, not the conscious mind (Luke 16:22-31; 23:43; Revelation 6:9-11). The believer who has died will be in God's presence (2 Corinthians 5:8; Philippians 1:23).

Question 9. One of the words that may come up in your discussion is the *Rapture*. This word is not found in the Bible, but it refers to Christ's taking his people to heaven at his return (1 Thessalonians 4:17). It comes from the Latin verb *rapire* meaning "to snatch" or "to seize." There is disagreement among Bible-believing Christians as to the time of the rapture of the church, so don't be surprised to find differences of opinion among your group. For the purposes of this study, it will be important to focus mainly on what Scripture actually says rather than on what participants may have heard on the subject in the past.

Regarding the order of events, the *Didache* or *The Teach-*

ing of the Twelve Apostles, a Christian book written about AD
95, lists three signs of the Second Coming: "First the sign of an
opening in heaven [referring to Revelation 6:14], then the sign
of the sound of the trumpet, and thirdly the resurrection of the
dead" (*Didache* 16:6).

Study 5: The Resurrection of the Dead

Question 5. First Corinthians 15:29 is one of the most puzzling
verses in the New Testament. The most widely held view is
that Christians were being baptized on behalf of believers who
had died before being baptized.

Question 6. The expression "firstfruits" in 1 Corinthians 15:20
refers to the fact that the whole harvest was anticipated and
consecrated by presenting the first stalks of grain as an offering
to God following the Passover meal on the day after the Sab-
bath (Leviticus 23:4-14). In other words, they were to offer
their firstfruits on the day that now corresponds with Easter,
Jesus's resurrection day! Christ's resurrection as the firstfruits
guarantees the resurrection of the rest of God's harvest (see
Matthew 13:37-39; Revelation 14:14-16). For further study of
firstfruits, see G. Colman Luck, "Firstfruits," *Wycliffe Bible Encyclopedia,* (Chicago: Moody, 1975, 1:610-611).

Question 11. In Genesis 1:28 Adam and Eve were ruling over
the kingdom of the world for God. But then, in Genesis 3:1-
6, Adam and Eve switched their allegiance from God to Satan,
accepting Satan's explanation of the world over God's. In
switching their allegiance, they took their kingdom with them
and gave it to Satan (Luke 4:6). This left God with two great

challenges that became his two main purposes throughout the Bible: (1) to reestablish his kingdom over the earth, and (2) to subdue his enemies.

STUDY 6: GOD'S PLAN FOR ISRAEL

Question 2. The Jews of Jesus's day knew from which tribe they had descended. Paul was a descendent of Benjamin, which along with the tribe of Judah comprised the southern kingdom (see also Philippians 3:5). Judah was the surviving nation after the northern kingdom of Israel was taken captive by Assyria in 722 BC.

Question 4. Jews are the descendants of the twelve sons of Jacob (Israel). Gentiles are all those who have not descended from Jacob.

In Jesus's parable of the vineyard tenants in Matthew 21:33-46, he illustrated how the Jews and their leaders first killed the prophets and then killed the son and heir. The application that Jesus made to his Jewish audience was that "the kingdom of God will be taken away from you and given to a people [the Gentiles] who will produce its fruit" (Matthew 21:43). In other words, because the Jews rejected their Messiah, the kingdom was taken from them and given to the Gentiles. Paul picked up on this as well in Romans 11:11-16.

Question 7. "The full number of the Gentiles" (Romans 11:25) is generally understood to refer to the final total number of Gentile believers, from the first coming of Christ to his second coming.

Question 8. The first three lines of the quotation in Romans 11:26-27 are taken from the Septuagint translation of Isaiah 59:20-21. (The Septuagint is the Greek translation of the Hebrew Old Testament from which the New Testament writers frequently quoted.) The Septuagint of Isaiah 59:20-21 states, "And the deliverer shall come for Zion's sake, and shall turn away ungodliness from Jacob. And this shall be my covenant with them."

The main difference between Paul's quotation in Romans 11:26, the Hebrew Old Testament, and the Septuagint is that Paul said "from Zion," the Old Testament Hebrew says "to Zion," and the Septuagint says "for Zion's sake." Paul was probably quoting the expression "from Zion" from Psalms 14:7 and 53:6, which both state, "Oh, that salvation for Israel would come out of Zion!"

The final phrase of Romans 11:27, "when I take away their sins," is a paraphrase of Isaiah 27:9. For further discussion of these verses, see James D. G. Dunn, *Word Biblical Commentary: Romans 9–16,* vol. 38b (Dallas: Word, 1988, pp. 682-684).

Question 9. The pouring out of the Spirit on the Day of Pentecost was a pouring "on all people" (Acts 2:17). This was the beginning of the age in which the gospel will go to *all* the nations (Matthew 28:19-20), whereas in Zechariah 12:10, the Spirit is poured out on "the house of David and the inhabitants of Jerusalem."

Question 10. Matthew 24:30 also uses the language of Zechariah 12:10.

Study 7: The Day of the Lord and the Wrath of God

Question 2. The Old Testament records "days of the Lord" against the Ammonites (Ezekiel 21:28-29), Babylon (Jeremiah 50:27,30-31), Damascus (Jeremiah 49:26), Edom (Isaiah 34:8-9), Egypt (Jeremiah 46:10), Moab (Jeremiah 48:41), the Philistines (Jeremiah 47:4), and Tyre (Isaiah 23:15). God will also have a day against Israel (Jeremiah 30:7). All of these days of the Lord point forward to the final Day of the Lord (2 Peter 3:7-13). This will be "the great day of...wrath" (Revelation 6:17).

Question 3. In study 4 we examined Paul's account of the resurrection of the dead and the rapture of the church in 1 Thessalonians 4:13-18. The verses in 1 Thessalonians 5 are a continuation of that discussion.

There are four verses in the Bible that speak of Jesus's coming "like a thief": First Thessalonians 5:2, 2 Peter 3:10, Revelation 3:3, and Revelation 16:15. The first two refer to the coming of the Day of the Lord, the second two to the Second Coming of Christ. It may be valuable to look at these for further light on the relationship of the Day of the Lord to the Second Coming of Christ. Compare also Matthew 24:42-43.

Question 5. The word *rebellion* in 2 Thessalonians 2:3 is a translation of the Greek word *apostasia* and can mean either "rebellion" or, when used in a religious sense, "apostasy"—an abandonment of the true faith (Arndt and Gingrich, *A Greek Lexicon,* p. 98). Thus, it can either be referring to the rebellion of the Antichrist or an associated departure from the true faith.

STUDY 8: THE BATTLE OF ARMAGEDDON

Question 2. The location to which God gathers the nations is called "the Valley of Jehoshaphat" (Joel 3:2,12), though there is no known valley by that name. However, the name *Jehoshaphat* means "Jehovah (or Yahweh) has judged." Since both verses where "the valley of Jehoshaphat" is used also mention God judging the nations (Joel 3:2,12), it is likely that the reference is to the valley of God's judgment rather than to a specific geographical location. For a fuller discussion of the Valley of Jehoshaphat, see J. A. Thompson, "Jehoshaphat, Valley of," *New Bible Dictionary,* 2nd ed. (Downers Grove, IL: InterVarsity, 1982, p. 557).

Question 6. The word *Armageddon* is a transliteration of the Hebrew words *Har Mageddon. Mageddon* stands for the ancient city of "Megiddo," while *har* can mean either "hill" or "mountain." Megiddo is located approximately eighteen miles southeast of the modern Israeli port of Haifa and ten miles south of Nazareth.

Specifically, Megiddo is located in the Jezreel Valley not far from where the brook of Nahal Iron enters the valley. Along this brook was one of the most important international trade routes of the ancient Near East. Because the narrow valley of Nahal Iron was the easiest place to control this route to the sea, Megiddo has been a strategic military location and the site of many battles throughout history.

Two battles recorded in the Bible were fought there. Deborah and Barak defeated Sisera at Megiddo (Judges 5:19). Later, King Josiah of Judah was killed in battle by Pharaoh Neco at Megiddo (2 Kings 23:29). For a fuller discussion of

Megiddo, see David Ussishkin, "Meggido," *The Anchor Bible Dictionary* (New York: Doubleday, 1992, IV: 666-679).

Question 9. It may be helpful to note that the outcome of the "great supper of God" in Revelation 19:17-21 corresponds with one of the curses on those who had broken God's covenant: Their corpses would be eaten by birds of prey (see Deuteronomy 28:26; see also Jeremiah 7:33; 16:4; 19:7; 34:20).

STUDY 9: THE JUDGMENT SEAT OF CHRIST

Question 3. A judgment seat was a tribunal, a seat on a raised platform for a judge. Christ will sit on God's judgment seat, and every believer will appear before him (Matthew 16:27; 25:31-46; Romans 14:10-12). In this study we will learn about this awesome event for Christians. In study 11 we will focus on the judgment of unbelievers.

Question 6. In the ancient world, ordeals were used as a common judicial procedure in every nation except China and Egypt. One of the most frequent ordeal elements was fire. For example, an accused person would be forced to walk over hot coals. If he was burned, that meant he was guilty. If he was not burned, that meant he was innocent. In the Bible, Shadrach, Meshach, and Abednego were found innocent in a fire ordeal (Daniel 3:13-30), whereas the 250 men who joined Korah's rebellion were found guilty in a similar ordeal (Numbers 16:35). Does 1 Corinthians 3:12-15 picture a fire ordeal?

Study 10: The Millennium

Question 1. The word *millennium* is derived from the Latin words *mille,* meaning "one thousand" and *anni,* meaning "years." According to Revelation 20, during the thousand years, Satan will be bound, and the saints will reign with Christ.

Premillennialists usually understand this to be a literal thousand-year period, while post- and amillennialists tend to view it metaphorically as a long period of time. Which view makes the most sense to you?

Question 3. Premillennialists believe that Satan's binding follows the battle described in Revelation 19:11-21. Post- and amillennialists generally understand Revelation 20 to be a summary of what has been described earlier, thus making the battle in 20:7-9 the same as the one recorded in 19:11-21.

Question 4. The *Abyss* in the New Testament is pictured as a subterranean location where demons are held against their will. The Greek word can also mean "depth" or "underworld" (see Luke 8:31; Revelation 9:1; 20:3).

Question 7. One view is that the first resurrection occurs at the second coming of Christ (1 Thessalonians 4:16). An alternate view is that it occurs at a person's conversion, when God makes us alive when we were "dead in transgressions" (Ephesians 2:5). Which interpretation makes sense to you?

Question 10. In Revelation 20:8, the phrase "Gog and Magog" is used to describe "the nations in the four corners of the earth" that gather to fight against God's people. In Ezekiel 38–39, there is an extended prophecy against "Gog, of the land of Magog."

STUDY 11: THE FINAL JUDGMENT

Question 5. The Book of Life (Philippians 4:3; Revelation 3:5; 13:8; 17:8; 20:12,15; 21:27) apparently is the register containing the names of the citizens of the kingdom of God. The books out of which men are judged show that God records the events in his kingdom as earthly kings also do.

Question 6. Hades is the place of the dead and is the Greek equivalent of the Hebrew term *Sheol.* For a description of Hades, read the story of the rich man and Lazarus in Luke 16:19-31. Whereas Lazarus is at "Abraham's side," the rich man is in hell (the Greek word *Hades*). What can we learn about Hades from this account?

Question 7. In Revelation 20:13 "death and Hades" are personified as they also are in Revelation 6:8. First Corinthians 15:26 says, "the last enemy to be destroyed is death," and this prediction is fulfilled in this scene. Death is an enemy in and of itself.

Question 10. Differences of interpretation of this passage among Christians are usually related to their views of the Millennium. Premillennialists typically understand these verses to refer to a judgment of unbelievers following the Millennium. Amillennialists and postmillennialists usually interpret it to be the judgment associated with the second coming of Christ (see appendix A).

STUDY 12: THE NEW HEAVEN AND THE NEW EARTH

Question 2. See Hebrews 12:22-24 and Revelation 21:2 for further information on the New Jerusalem. See 1 John 5:5 for more on the overcomers who will inherit heaven.

Question 4. The nation of Israel was built upon the twelve tribes of the sons of Jacob (Israel), while the church has been built on the foundation of Christ's twelve apostles (Ephesians 2:20).

Question 5. The shape of the New Jerusalem is a cube 1,400 miles by 1,400 miles by 1,400 miles. In other words, it is a huge version of the most holy places of the ancient tabernacle and temple, which also were cubes (see 1 Kings 6:20). The most holy place—the Holy of Holies—served as God's throne room, where he dwelt in the midst of his people (Exodus 40:34-35; 1 Kings 8:10-13). God will dwell with his people forever in the new Holy City.

Question 7. Helpful questions to ask in trying to understand the identity of the nations and kings of Revelation 21:24–22:2 are: What would have happened if Adam and Eve had not sinned? What would the fulfillment of Genesis 1:28 look like in comparison to Revelation 21–22?

Views of End-Times Events

The Millennium: The thousand-Year Reign of Christ over the Earth

Premillennialism
The view that Christ will return before the Millennium.

	Second Coming	
Church Age	Millennium	Eternal State

Postmillennialism
The view that Christ will return after the Millennium.

		Second Coming	
(1)	Church Age	Millennium	Eternal State

		Second Coming	
(2)	Church Age = Millennium		Eternal State

Amillennialism
The view that there will be no Millennium.

	Second Coming	
Church Age		Eternal State

Bibliography and Resources

General

Archer, Gleason, Paul Feinberg, Douglas Moo, and Richard
   Reiter. *Three Views on the Rapture:
   Pre-, Mid-, and Post-Tribulation?* Grand Rapids: Zon-
   dervan, 1996.
Clouse, Robert G., ed. *The Meaning of the Millennium: Four
   Views.* Downers Grove, IL: InterVarsity, 1977.
Lightner, Robert P. *The Last Days Handbook: A Comprehen-
   sive Guide to Understanding the Different Views of
   Prophecy. Who Believes What About Prophecy and Why.*
   Nashville: Nelson, 1990.

Amillennial

Poythress, Vern. *Understanding Dispensationalists.* Phillipsburg, NJ: Presbyterian and Reformed Publishing Company, 1993.
Vos, Geerhardus. *The Pauline Eschatology.* Grand Rapids:
   Eerdmans, 1961.

Pretribulational Premillennial

McClain, Alva J. *The Greatness of the Kingdom.* Winona
   Lake, IN: B.M.H. Books, 1959.
Pentecost, J. Dwight. *Things to Come.* Grand Rapids:
   Zondervan, 1965.

POST-TRIBULATIONAL PREMILLENNIAL

Ladd, George Eldon. *The Blessed Hope*. Grand Rapids: Eerdmans, 1956.

————. *The Presence of the Future: The Eschatology of Biblical Realism*. Grand Rapids: Eerdmans, 1974.

POSTMILLENNIAL

Chilton, David. *Paradise Restored: A Biblical Theology of
Dominion*. Tyler, TX: Reconstruction Press, 1985.

Kik, J. Marcellus. *An Eschatology of Victory*. Phillipsburg, NJ:
Presbyterian and Reformed Publishing Company, 1974.

What Should We Study Next?

If you enjoyed this Fisherman Bible Studyguide, you might want to explore our full line of Fisherman Resources and Bible Studyguides. The following books offer time-tested Fisherman inductive Bible studies for individuals or groups.

FISHERMAN RESOURCES

The Art of Spiritual Listening: Responding to God's Voice Amid the Noise of Life by Alice Fryling

Balm in Gilead by Dudley Delffs

The Essential Bible Guide by Whitney T. Kuniholm

Questions from the God Who Needs No Answers: What Is He Really Asking of You? by Carolyn and Craig Williford

Reckless Faith: Living Passionately As Imperfect Christians by Jo Kadlecek

Soul Strength: Spiritual Courage for the Battles of Life by Pam Lau

FISHERMAN BIBLE STUDYGUIDES

Topical Studies

Angels by Vinita Hampton Wright

Becoming Women of Purpose by Ruth Haley Barton

Building Your House on the Lord: A Firm Foundation for Family Life (Revised Edition) by Steve and Dee Brestin

Discipleship: The Growing Christian's Lifestyle by James and
    Martha Reapsome
*Doing Justice, Showing Mercy: Christian Action in Today's
    World* by Vinita Hampton Wright
Encouraging Others: Biblical Models for Caring by Lin Johnson
The End Times: Discovering What the Bible Says by E. Michael
    Rusten
Examining the Claims of Jesus by Dee Brestin
Friendship: Portraits in God's Family Album by Steve and Dee
    Brestin
The Fruit of the Spirit: Cultivating Christlike Character by
    Stuart Briscoe
Great Doctrines of the Bible by Stephen Board
Great Passages of the Bible by Carol Plueddemann
Great Prayers of the Bible by Carol Plueddemann
Growing Through Life's Challenges by James and Martha
    Reapsome
Guidance & God's Will by Tom and Joan Stark
Heart Renewal: Finding Spiritual Refreshment by Ruth Goring
Higher Ground: Steps Toward Christian Maturity by Steve and
    Dee Brestin
Images of Redemption: God's Unfolding Plan Through the Bible
    by Ruth E. Van Reken
Integrity: Character from the Inside Out by Ted W. Engstrom
    and Robert C. Larson
Lifestyle Priorities by John White
Marriage: Learning from Couples in Scripture by R. Paul and
    Gail Stevens
Miracles by Robbie Castleman
One Body, One Spirit: Building Relationships in the Church by
    Dale and Sandy Larsen

The Parables of Jesus by Gladys Hunt

Parenting with Purpose and Grace: Wisdom for Responding to Your Child's Deepest Needs by Alice Fryling

Prayer: Discovering What Scripture Says by Timothy Jones and Jill Zook-Jones

The Prophets: God's Truth Tellers by Vinita Hampton Wright

Proverbs and Parables: God's Wisdom for Living by Dee Brestin

Satisfying Work: Christian Living from Nine to Five by R. Paul Stevens and Gerry Schoberg

Senior Saints: Growing Older in God's Family by James and Martha Reapsome

The Sermon on the Mount: The God Who Understands Me by Gladys M. Hunt

Speaking Wisely: Exploring the Power of Words by Poppy Smith

Spiritual Disciplines: The Tasks of a Joyful Life by Larry Sibley

Spiritual Gifts by Karen Dockrey

Spiritual Hunger: Filling Your Deepest Longings by Jim and Carol Plueddemann

A Spiritual Legacy: Faith for the Next Generation by Chuck and Winnie Christensen

Spiritual Warfare: Disarming the Enemy Through the Power of God by A. Scott Moreau

The Ten Commandments: God's Rules for Living by Stuart Briscoe

Ultimate Hope for Changing Times by Dale and Sandy Larsen

When Faith Is All You Have: A Study of Hebrews 11 by Ruth E. Van Reken

Where Your Treasure Is: What the Bible Says About Money by James and Martha Reapsome

Who Is God? by David P. Seemuth

Who Is Jesus? In His Own Words by Ruth E. Van Reken

Who Is the Holy Spirit? by Barbara H. Knuckles and Ruth E.
  Van Reken
Wisdom for Today's Woman: Insights from Esther by Poppy
  Smith
Witnesses to All the World: God's Heart for the Nations by Jim
  and Carol Plueddemann
Women at Midlife: Embracing the Challenges by Jeanie Miley
Worship: Discovering What Scripture Says by Larry Sibley

Bible Book Studies

Genesis: Walking with God by Margaret Fromer and Sharrel
  Keyes
Exodus: God Our Deliverer by Dale and Sandy Larsen
Ruth: Relationships That Bring Life by Ruth Haley Barton
Ezra and Nehemiah: A Time to Rebuild by James Reapsome
(For Esther, see Topical Studies, *Wisdom for Today's Woman*)
Job: Trusting Through Trials by Ron Klug
Psalms: A Guide to Prayer and Praise by Ron Klug
Proverbs: Wisdom That Works by Vinita Hampton Wright
Ecclesiastes: A Time for Everything by Stephen Board
Song of Songs: A Dialogue of Intimacy by James Reapsome
Jeremiah: The Man and His Message by James Reapsome
Jonah, Habakkuk, and Malachi: Living Responsibly by Margaret Fromer and Sharrel Keyes
Matthew: People of the Kingdom by Larry Sibley
Mark: God in Action by Chuck and Winnie Christensen
Luke: Following Jesus by Sharrel Keyes
John: An Eyewitness Account of the Son of God by Whitney T.
  Kuniholm
Acts 1–12: God Moves in the Early Church by Chuck and
  Winnie Christensen

Acts 13–28, see *Paul* under Character Studies
Romans: The Christian Story by James Reapsome
1 Corinthians: Problems and Solutions in a Growing Church by
    Charles and Ann Hummel
Strengthened to Serve: 2 Corinthians by Jim and Carol
    Plueddemann
Galatians, Titus, and Philemon: Freedom in Christ by Whitney
    Kuniholm
Ephesians: Living in God's Household by Robert Baylis
Philippians: God's Guide to Joy by Ron Klug
Colossians: Focus on Christ by Luci Shaw
Letters to the Thessalonians by Margaret Fromer and Sharrel
    Keyes
Letters to Timothy: Discipleship in Action by Margaret Fromer
    and Sharrel Keyes
Hebrews: Foundations for Faith by Gladys Hunt
James: Faith in Action by Chuck and Winnie Christensen
1 and 2 Peter, Jude: Called for a Purpose by Steve and Dee
    Brestin
1, 2, 3 John: How Should a Christian Live? by Dee Brestin
Revelation: The Lamb Who Is the Lion by Gladys Hunt

Bible Character Studies
Abraham: Model of Faith by James Reapsome
David: Man After God's Own Heart by Robbie Castleman
Elijah: Obedience in a Threatening World by Robbie
    Castleman
Great People of the Bible by Carol Plueddemann
King David: Trusting God for a Lifetime by Robbie Castleman
Men Like Us: Ordinary Men, Extraordinary God by Paul
    Heidebrecht and Ted Schcuermann

Moses: Encountering God by Greg Asimakoupoulos
Paul: Thirteenth Apostle (Acts 13–28) by Chuck and Winnie
    Christensen
Women Like Us: Wisdom for Today's Issues by Ruth Haley
    Barton
Women Who Achieved for God by Winnie Christensen
Women Who Believed God by Winnie Christensen